Saint Frideswi

SAINT FRIDESWIDE

PATRON OF OXFORD

The Earliest Texts
edited and introduced by

JOHN BLAIR

With wood engravings by

KATHLEEN LINDSLEY

THE PERPETUA PRESS

OXFORD

ISBN 1 870 882 17 2

Printed in Great Britain by
Oxuniprint, Oxford University Press
and distributed from 26 Norham Road
Oxford OX2 6SF

Contents

List of Illustrations

In memory of my grandfather

ARTHUR LEOPOLD DRINKWATER
1886–1985

of Pembroke College, Oxford
and rector of
Little Bookham, Surrey

-➤-<-

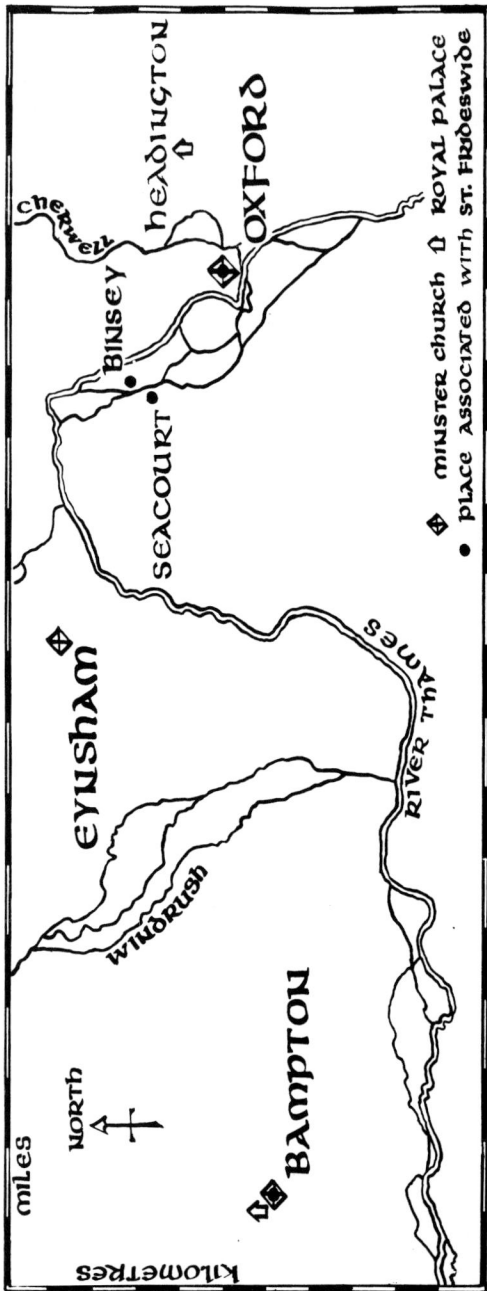

Introduction

It is virtually certain that Oxford developed around a
mid-Saxon monastic church (the predecessor of the present Cathedral) at a major crossing over the Thames, and
that the first head of the church was a princess named
Frideswide.[1] Beyond this, certainty fails. The traditions
about Frideswide were written down, in the form in
which we now have them, nearly four centuries after her
death, and are clearly much elaborated. The text of her
Life was dismissed in 1936 by the great historian Sir Frank
Stenton as practically worthless,[2] with the result that it
has received no scholarly study. Indeed, the earliest
known version of it was printed for the first time in 1988,
and the present translation into English is the first.

But the material is not quite so useless as Stenton
thought. His condemnation was based on a belief that the
Life was only written in the thirteenth century; the recog-
nition that it survives in a manuscript of c. 1130 re-opens
the whole question. Furthermore, the legend contains
elements which seem close enough to the world of mid-
Saxon England to command a degree of respect. The
difficulties and confusions are well worth unravelling, for
if St Frideswide's story preserves any reliable facts at all,
they are the earliest in the history of Oxford.

The legend

Only three sources deserve consideration, all of them written during the century or so after the Norman conquest:

(i) A brief narrative written c. 1125 by the historian William of Malmesbury (printed *Gesta Pontificum Anglorum*, ed. N.E.S.A. Hamilton (Rolls Ser. lii, London, 1870), p. 315) (Text I).

(ii) 'Life A', considerably longer than Malmesbury's narrative and including several miracle stories. It is written in a bald, rather clumsy Latin, often borrowing phrases from the Vulgate; Frideswide herself, who is said to know the Psalms by heart, quotes them copiously. The only full text is in a Worcester manuscript of c. 1130 (British Library MS Cotton Nero E 1 (ii) ff. 156–7ᵛ) (Text II).

(iii) 'Life B', a longer and more elegant re-working of Life A, almost certainly written c. 1140–70 by Robert of Cricklade, a notable Oxford scholar and Prior of St Frideswide's. The earliest copy is in a Pershore manuscript of c. 1170 (Bodleian Library MS Laud Misc. 114 ff. 132–40); two other manuscripts provide some variant readings. Despite its more elaborate style, Life B has few significant changes from Life A, and only one significant addition (Text III).

Malmesbury's story may be slightly, though only

slightly, earlier than the surviving manuscript of Life A. On the other hand, Life A seems to date, in the form in which we have it, from around 1110–20, and may incorporate substantial passages of older material. If, as seems likely, Malmesbury drew on the same lost source, his narrative and Life A are both primary evidence for its contents. Life B, by contrast, is largely derivative, although its one substantial addition may be based on a tradition independent of Life A.

Malmesbury's story is a very simple one. A princess named Frideswide is pursued, despite her monastic vows, by a young king madly in love with her. He chases her into a wood, from which she escapes to Oxford. The king follows her there, but she prays for divine protection and he is struck blind as he enters the town. Recognising the error of his ways, he begs Frideswide's forgiveness and regains his sight, leaving her in peace to found a monastery in Oxford where eventually she ends her days.

Life A is much more elaborate, and contains some important differences. Frideswide's parents are named as Didan king of Oxford and Sefrida his queen. Didan founds and endows the monastery, and Frideswide is consecrated as a nun to live there with twelve companions. Her suitor is Algar king of Leicester, not merely an over-persistent young man but a savage tyrant. He sends messengers to demand Frideswide's hand. When she refuses they try to seize her, are struck blind, repent, recover their sight, and report back to Algar, who sets out in person to take her. Warned by an angel, Frideswide goes to the Thames with two companions; they are met by an angelic boatman, who transports them up-river to Bampton where they hide in a swineherd's hut in 'a certain wood called Binsey'. Meanwhile Algar tries to enter Oxford and is struck blind, remaining, in this version, uncured and unrepentant for the rest of his days. Frideswide stays at Bampton for three years, working miraculous cures. The nuns then return by boat to Oxford, where Frideswide continues her life of prayer and abstinence. Eventually an angel warns her of her approaching death, which occurs, attended by visions and portents, on 19 October 727. The Life ends with two miracles during the funeral.

The central problem of this version is its gross confusion between Frideswide's two hiding-places. Binsey is not a wood in Bampton, thirteen miles west of Oxford, but lies less than two miles from the city. The possibility of a straightforward mistake—that a wood in Bampton had a name like Binsey and came to be confused with it—is ruled out by the miracles associated with this episode. The first, the healing of a blind girl, is explicitly located at Bampton. But the second subject is a young man of Seacourt, only 600 yards from Binsey church: obviously this miracle relates to the genuine Binsey. It must be concluded that there were separate legends of Frideswide at Bampton and at Binsey, both involving miracles, and that Life A has conflated and confused them.

If the author of Life A was ignorant of local geography,

the twelfth-century canons of St Frideswide's Priory were not. The confusion, which obviously diminished credibility in their foundation story, must have worried them: Prior Robert had the task of making Life B a more credible narrative as well as a more elegant one. He did this by inserting, between the first and second Bampton miracles, a new chapter which transports Frideswide from Bampton to Binsey in time to cure the young man of Seacourt (Text III). The nuns set out to re-join their sisters at Oxford, but as the boat nears the city Frideswide decides to stay at Binsey for a final spell of solitude. They find a lonely and overgrown spot called Thornbury where they build an oratory (the present St Margaret's chapel), and a healing well, still to be seen on the west side of the chapel, springs up in answer to Frideswide's prayers.

There was a good practical reason for introducing this well-known and well-loved story: in the twelfth century Binsey belonged to the Priory, which was obliged to defend its title against rival claims. But the existence of some sort of traditional association between Frideswide and Binsey is proved by Life A, and it may be that the author of Life B had access to further evidence. At all events, the confusions are themselves testimony to a body of tradition older than the post-Conquest sources now available.

The history behind the legend

To understand Frideswide in the context of her own times, it is necessary to consider the political and religious developments of the previous century. The first Germanic colonisers of the Upper Thames were the West Saxons, whose descendants preserved traditions of the capture of British strongholds at Benson and Eynsham.[3] Concentrations of excavated cemeteries and settlements prove that both places lay in areas of intensive activity during the pagan Anglo-Saxon period, and when, in 634, the West Saxons became Christian, their bishopric was established at Dorchester-on-Thames near the royal headquarters of Benson.[4] But meanwhile the Midland kingdom of Mercia was expanding under its great kings Penda (?626–55) and Wulfhere (658–75). By the presumed time of Frideswide's birth the territory around Oxford would have been under Mercian overlordship, and probably ruled, like other such dependencies, by a local sub-king.[5]

'King Didan' is thus an eminently plausible figure, though his kingdom need not necessarily have included the whole later county. If he only ruled in west Oxfordshire, his headquarters may well have been at the old centre of Eynsham. He is otherwise unknown, but placenames such as Deddington show that his name, presumably *Dida*, *Daeda* or *Dydda*, is a plausible one. 'Frideswide' (*Frithuswith*, 'Peace-Strong') is also an acceptable mid-

Saxon name, which might even suggest some relationship to the late seventh-century Mercian noblemen Frithuwold and Frithuric, or to the Frithugyth who was married to King Æthelheard of Wessex in the 730s. So the main characters are appropriate to their time and context.

The period c.650–720 was the great age of English monastic foundations, especially by kings and princes. On the contemporary Gallic pattern, many were 'double' houses of nuns and monks and were ruled by royal abbesses. For example, monasteries at Bicester and Aylesbury seem to have been established under the rule of Eadburh and Osgyth, repectively sister and niece of the Mercian over-king Wulfhere.[6] Such monasteries, unlike their later medieval successors, had parochial authority over their districts and probably maintained priests. The Oxford house is consistent with this pattern: founded by a Mercian sub-king, ruled by his daughter, and containing a community of nuns. Life A may preserve a memory of a double community in its statement that Didan 'assigned religious men to serve them'. The church is said to have been dedicated 'in honour of the Holy Trinity, the spotless Virgin Mary and All Saints', whereas Frideswide simply asks to be buried in St Mary's church; this inconsistency may possibly preserve a hint that the Oxford monastery, like others, had three churches with separate patron saints. Excavation has shown that there was a substantial graveyard on the site of Oxford cathedral from the late seventh century, and that the nearby

Thames crossing, presumably the original 'oxenford', was a major throughfare by the same date.[7]

The story of King Algar's pursuit is scarcely to be taken very seriously: the holy virgin persecuted by a lecherous prince, but then saved through divine intervention, is a stock figure of medieval hagiography. On the other hand, the abduction of noble ladies for dynastic ends was common early medieval practice, and King Æthelbald of Mercia, who began his reign eleven years before Frideswide's reputed death, was accused of seducing nuns. It is not inherently unlikely that something of the sort may have happened to Frideswide.

A more specific context can be suggested for the Bampton and Binsey episodes. In the late Anglo-Saxon period Bampton was an important royal centre, with its own monastic church and local saint.[8] A holy well west of the church, later noted for curing eye diseases,[9] is strikingly reminiscent of the Binsey legend. The traditional association of Frideswide with so inherently likely a place, where her monastery had no vested interests in inventing an association later, has the ring of truth.

At Binsey there are traces of a large oval enclosure, containing the churchyard, which probably began as a late Iron Age valley-fort. Excavations on its perimeter in 1987 found a sequence of boundary ditches beginning in the first century A.D. but associated with two sherds of seventh- or eighth- century pottery. If this was indeed a monastic settlement, its nearness to Oxford suggests that we may be dealing with a retreat-house used by the main community for periods of solitude. Such establishments certainly existed at the time: according to Bede, Bishop John of Hexham (687–706) had 'a more isolated house, surrounded by open woodland and a ditch, not far from Hexham church, that is almost a mile and a half . . ., in which the man of God used to retire with a few companions to pray and read quietly whenever he had the chance, and especially during Lent'.[10] The references to Binsey in Life A and Life B suggest similar activities in a similar setting.

ST MARY'S CHURCH BAMPTON

Oxford lies six miles east of Eynsham, Bampton eight miles west. As well as being an early secular centre Eynsham had an important monastic church, first mentioned in 864, with estates which were in two cases adjacent to those of St Frideswide's monastery.[11] Possibly Eynsham was the 'head minister' of this little kingdom, with other religious communities at Oxford and Bampton. Oxford, like Bampton, may have had a royal palace, perhaps already on the later site at Headington. Such a scheme links the two main places in Frideswide's legend, with the king's daughter travelling along the main thoroughfare of the Thames from one royal centre to another.

A reasonable guess at the true story, demythologised and interpreted in the context of its times, would be something like this: In the late seventh century a territory west of the Cherwell and north of the Thames was ruled, under the overlordship of Mercia, by a sub-king called Dida. His kingdom probably included both Bampton and Oxford, though his headquarters may have been at the already ancient centre of Eynsham. Following contemporary fashion, he built and endowed at Oxford a double monastery, possibly dependent on a slightly older and more important monastery at Eynsham, and made his daughter Frithuswith its first abbess. She spent part of her life at two other religious centres in her father's kingdom: Bampton, later recorded as a royal vill and minster church, and Binsey, much nearer to Oxford, which may have been attached to her own community. She died on 19 October 727 and was buried in her monastery, which became the nucleus of the nascent town of Oxford.

The later history of Frideswide's monastery and relics

Like many double monasteries, Frideswide's seems to
have evolved during the ninth and tenth centuries into a
'secular' minster: a community neither of nuns nor of
strict monks, but one of priests living with their families
and probably engaged in pastoral work. A glimpse of it is
afforded by king Æthelred the Unready's charter
describing the notorious 'St Brice's Day Massacre' of
1002:[12]

In the year of the incarnation of our Lord 1004, the second
indiction, in the 25th year of my reign, by the ordering of
God's providence, I, Æthelred, governing the monarchy of all
Albion, have made secure with the liberty of a privilege by the
royal authority a certain monastery situated in the town which
is called Oxford, where the body of the blessed Frideswide
rests, for the love of the all-accomplishing God; and I have
restored the territories which belong to that monastery of
Christ with the renewal of a new title-deed; and I will relate in
a few words to all who look upon this document for what
reason it was done. For it is fully agreed that to all dwelling in
this country it will be well known that, since a decree was sent
out by me with the counsel of my leading men and magnates,
to the effect that all the Danes who had sprung up in this
island, sprouting like cockle amongst the wheat, were to be
destroyed by a most just extermination, and this decree was to
be put into effect even as far as death, those Danes who dwelt

in the afore-mentioned town, striving to escape death, entered the sanctuary of Christ, having broken by force the doors and bolts, and resolved to make a refuge and defence for themselves therein against the people of the town and the suburbs; but when all the people in pursuit strove, forced by necessity, to drive them out, and could not, they set fire to the planks and burnt, as it seems, this church with its ornaments and books. Afterwards, with God's aid, it was renewed by me and my subjects, and, as I have said above, strengthened by Christ's name with the honour of a fresh privilege along with the territories belonging to it, and endowed with every liberty, regarding royal exactions as well as ecclesiastical dues.

Otherwise we know nothing of the eleventh-century community beyond the statement that 'St Frideswide rests at Oxford' in a late Anglo-Saxon list, and Domesday Book's record of 'the land of the canons of Oxford' in 1086.[13] By the 1100s ecclesiastical opinion looked with disfavour upon such 'irregular' houses of priests, and St Frideswide was reformed, like so many others, as a priory of canons regular following the Augustinian rule.[14]

In an age which was coming once again to value the Anglo-Saxon saints, it is not surprising that the canons should have wished to raise their patron's body into a worthier shrine. Unfortunately, they were not completely sure where it lay. According to Life A, Frideswide was originally buried on the south side of her church. Life B adds that after the fire King Æthelred enlarged the church in such a way that the grave was thereafter central. A narrative preserved in a fourteeth-century manuscript[15] describes how Abingdon Abbey had held the church between the expulsion of the secular clerks and the installation of the Augustinians—a fact which aroused fears that the Abingdon monks had stolen the precious corpse. An investigation, vividly described in the same text, was therefore carried out at some date between the 1110s and 1180. After fasting for three days, the canons entered the church secretly at dead of night and began to excavate the grave by torchlight. Finding an empty stone coffin they almost despaired, 'but urged by an astute man amongst them they set about digging deeper. For he said that it had once been a common practice to put empty coffins over the bodies of saints, so that if thieves came intent on stealing the body they would go away deluded'. Thus encouraged, the excavators continued until they found a skeleton, whereupon all their torches were miraculously extinguished and re-kindled. Convinced by this heaven-sent sign that they had indeed found Frideswide, they closed the grave and left the corpse in peace.

'Thererafter', continues the narrative, 'miracles started to come thicker than before, and the virgin's grave was visited more diligently by people from many parts'. Prior Philip decided to enhance his house's prestige by a solemn 'translation' of the relics into a raised shrine, accompanied by the maximum publicity.[16] The ceremony took place on 12 February 1180, when the Archbishop of Canterbury and other notables were in Oxford attending a royal council. The party came into the church, and then the Archbishop 'opened with the greatest reverence the grave in which her most blessed corpse had rested for nearly 480 years. With a great crowd of clergy and people standing round and rejoicing, he took the virgin's glorious bones from the grave and laid them in a feretory fittingly embellished for this purpose, so that so precious a pearl, who proclaimed her life in heaven by such glorious miracles, should lie no longer hidden in the earth. Then the bystanders were filled with a most delightful scent which refreshed them like spices, so that it seemed not inappropriate to say of her, "The smell of thine ointments is above all manner of spices".' Nor did Frideswide disappoint her devotees. Nearly a hundred miracles followed in rapid succession, and were recorded in a treatise by the enterprising Prior Philip.[17] To judge from this collection, disturbed adolescent girls were especially prominent amongst the saint's clientele.

Frideswide's bones were translated into a better shrine in 1289,[18] but her cult in the later middle ages does not seem to have lived up to its early promise. Nonetheless, it survived until the general destruction of the Reformation engulfed it. The Priory was suppressed, and in 1546 its church became the Cathedral of the new diocese of Oxford. Frideswide's shrine was destroyed in the late 1530s, and the bones buried on its site. The bizarre events which followed are recounted in a treatise published in 1561 by James Calfhill, canon of Christ Church.[19] Catherine Martyr, wife of the Protestant reformer Peter Martyr, was buried near 'Frideswide's tomb' in 1552. A year later the Catholic Queen Mary came to the throne, and in 1556 her commissioners directed that Catherine's body should be exhumed and buried in a dunghill. At the same time, it seems, Frideswide's bones were also disinterred and placed in two silk bags. In 1562 another team of commissioners, sent by Queen Elizabeth, ordered the return of Catherine Martyr to seemly Christian burial. Calfhill then describes the arrangements which he made for her second funeral:

Then I called together all those who had been parties to the outrage, or its agents, or at least had good reason to know the rightful place of the holy monument and the wretched details of its shameful violation. I was taken to Frideswide's tomb and shown where the grave had been, not far from it on the north side of the church . . . Meanwhile, as my office required, I was carefully making all the necessary arrangements for a worthy funeral; and I happened to find, in the obscurest part of the church, some dingy bones carefully wrapped up and preserved in two silk bags. The foolish old canons of the house had been used to guard them religiously, and at the more solemn feasts to place them publicly on the altar in the sight of all for the ignorant multitude to worship with the utmost reverence and honour. For the old belief was that they were the virgin Frideswide's. Such power and holiness was ascribed to them by crazy old men, and people deluded by Popish auguries, that they exclaimed that the fabric of the church would fall in utter ruin if they were removed from the place. Since I hold that nothing less becomes a good man than to copy hateful Popish sacrilege and barbarous cruelty, I was determined on no account to let anything unseemly or insulting be done with them. So I hit upon a scheme by which the bones could be dealt with decently, while at the same time all foolish superstition could be suppressed. So, after a sermon telling the people the reasons for my choice, they were buried mingled and confused with the bones of Peter Martyr's wife in the upper part of the church towards the east, in the same monument, much honoured and frequented by men, on 11 January 1561.

The site of this burial cannot be certainly located. In any case, it is impossible to know whether the bones found in the twelfth century were really Frideswide's, whether her body was taken to Abingdon, or whether it still lies undisturbed in her original grave. But large pieces of the thirteenth-century shrine were discovered in a well in 1875 and replaced in the cathedral.[20] By a lucky chance, further fragments were found in 1985 during the same excavations which revealed the Anglo-Saxon cemetery, and yet more turned up in the cathedral store. During 2002, all the extant pieces were cleaned, conserved, and built into a much more complete reconstruction. This is on a new site in the Latin Chapel, close to where the shrine probably stood in the late middle ages, and in front of Burne-Jones's magnificent window with its scenes from the saint's life. It now provides a rather more worthy monument to the eighth-century princess around whose remains have grown the City and University of Oxford.

CHRIST CHURCH CATHEDRAL

Note on the texts and translations

The texts of Lives A and B are edited, and their contents much more fully discussed, in J. Blair, 'Saint Frideswide Reconsidered', *Oxoniensa*, lii (1987), 71–127. The present introduction is a summary of the conclusions presented there. The translation of Life A is based on the text in British Library MS Cotton Nero E1, with a few preferred readings from a later summary in British Library MS Lansdowne 436. Quotations from the Bible are indicated by use of single inverted commas (as distinct from the double inverted commas used for reported speech).

Notes

1. For Oxford's Anglo-Saxon origins, now see: A. Dodd (ed.), *Oxford Before the University* (Oxford, 2003).

2. F. M. Stenton, 'St Frideswide and her Times', *Oxoniensia*, i (1936), 103–12. For a more recent (but very misleading) assessment of the evidence, see E. F. Jacob, *St Frideswide, the Patron Saint of Oxford* (Oxford, 1957).

3. *Anglo-Saxon Chronicle*, s.a. 571 (The attribution of this annal to 571 is probably arbitrary, and the date seems likely to be much too late).

4. G. Briggs, J. Cook and T. Rowley (eds.), *The Archaeology of the Oxford Region* (Oxford, 1986), map 11; *Baedae Opera Historica*, ed. C. Plummer (Oxford, 1896), i, 139.

5. See for instance J. Campbell, 'Bede's *Reges* and *Principes*', in his *Essays in Anglo-Saxon History* (London, 1986), 85–98.

6. See C. Hohler, 'St Osyth and Aylesbury', *Records of Buckinghamshire*, xviii (1966–70), 61–72.

7. Burials found in 1985 in excavations by C. Scull in the Cathedral cloister have produced radiocarbon dates from the eighth to tenth centuries (published in *Oxoniensia*, liii (1988), 60-2); other burials from the same cemetery were found in 1972 in Tom Quad (*Oxoniensia*, xxxviii (1973), 270–4). For the river-crossing see B. Durham, 'Archaeological Excavations in St Aldate's, Oxford', *Oxoniensia*, xlii (1977), 83–203; B. Durham, 'The Thames Crossing at Oxford', *Oxoniensia*, xlix (1984), 57–100.

8. J. Blair, 'Saint Beornwald of Bampton', *Oxoniensia*, xlix (1984), 47–55.

9. J. Blair, *Bampton Folklore* (2001), 37–9.

10. *Baedae Opera Historica*, ed. C. Plummer (Oxford 1896), i, 283; cf. E. Cambridge in *Journal of British Archaeological Association*, cxxxvii (1984), 76–7. For the Binsey enclosure see *Oxoniensia*, liii (1988), 3–20.

11. Shipton-on-Cherwell with Whitehill, Water Eaton with Cutteslowe: see P. H. Sawyer, *Anglo Saxon Charters: An Annotated List and*

Bibliography (London, 1968), Nos 210, 909, 911; the 864 reference to Eynsham minster is in Ibid. No. 210.

12. Ibid., No. 909: translation from D. Whitelock, *English Historical Documents: I: c. 500–1042* (2nd edn., London, 1979), 590–3.

13. F. Liebermann, *Die Heiligen Englands* (Hanover, 1889); *Victoria History of the County of Oxfordshire, i* (London, 1939), 409.

14. For the Augustinian Priory see J. Blair, 'St Frideswide's Monastery', *Oxoniensia, liii* (1988) 221–58, at 226–42.

15. British Library, MS Lansdowne 436 ff. 103–4; printed *Oxoniensia, lii* (1987), 117–18.

16. The following account is from Prior Philip's miracle collection, Bodleian Library, MS Digby 177 ff. 1ᵛ–2, printed *Oxoniensia, lii* (1987), 118–19.

17. Bodlean Library, MS Digby 177: discussed by H. Mayr-Harting, 'The Miracles of St Frideswide', in H. Mayr-Harting and R. I. Moore (eds.), *Studies in Medieval History Presented to R. H. C. Davis* (London, 1985), 193–206.

18. J. C. Wall, *Shrines of British Saints* (London 1905), 64–71; N. Coldstream, 'English Decorated Shrine Bases', *Journal of the British Archaeological Association, cxxix* (1976), 17.

19. J. Calfhill, *Historia de Catharinae uxoris D. Petri Martyris Piisimae Exhumatione, ac Eiusdem ad Honestam Sepulturam Restitutione, Anno MDLXI* (1561) (my translation).

20. Wall op cit. note 18, 66–8.

I

William of Malmesbury's Summary

(c. 1125)

In old times there was in the city of Oxford a monastery of nuns, where rests the most holy virgin Frideswide. A king's daughter, she spurned a king's bed, avowing her chastity to the Lord Christ. But the king had set his heart upon marrying the virgin, and when prayers and flatteries had been spent in vain he prepared to take her by force. Frideswide learnt of this and fled into a wood. No refuge could be secret from the lover, no coldness of heart could deter him: he followed the fugitive. So once again, when the young man's frenzy became plain, with God's help she entered Oxford at dead of night by means of hidden ways. By morning the persistent lover had hastened there too, and the girl, now despairing of flight and too weary to go any further, prayed to God for protection for herself and punishment for her persecutor. As he passed through the town gates with his thegns, a heaven-sent blow struck him blind. Understanding the wrongfulness of his persistence, he placated Frideswide by means of messengers and recovered his sight as quickly as he had lost it. Thus it came about that kings of England are afraid to enter or lodge in that town: it is said to bring ruin, and they all shrink from the danger of putting it to the test. So the woman, secure in her maidenly victory, established a monastery there where she ended her days, submitting to her bridegroom's call.

In the time of king Æthelred, the Danes, doomed to be slain, fled into that monastery and were consumed by fire together with the buildings through the insatiable anger of the English. But soon the sanctuary was purified by the king's penance, the monastery rebuilt, old lands returned, new possessions added. In our own time only a few clerks remained there, who lived as they pleased, so Roger bishop of Salisbury gave the place to Wimund, a canon of excellent learning and no mean holiness. He, toiling fruitfully at the task entrusted to him, established there for God many canons to live according to the rule.

II

The Early Twelfth-Century Life
('Life A')

When the English people had been taught and baptized
through blessed Augustine's preaching, priests and
deacons were appointed, and churches were built and
dedicated throughout the nation. So 'the multitude of
believers grew', and through the whole land of the
English the church abounded with new offsping.

Long afterwards there was a king of Oxford named
Didan. He took a wife named Sefrida, a godly woman
diligent in all good works. They rejoiced together in the
flower of their youth, and the Lord made them fruitful. So
revered Sefrida conceived, and in due time produced a
daughter. When the king heard this he rejoiced greatly,
and ordered that she should be re-born with water and
the Holy Spirit.

So she was baptized, and they called her Frideswide.
This king's daughter was carefully brought up, and after
five years they entrusted her to a woman called Ælfgifu to
learn her letters. The maiden, whom God was already

preparing to be a vessel of the Holy Spirit, so applied herself to her studies that within six months she knew the whole Psalter. So the blessed virgin Frideswide 'grew from strength to strength', striving wholeheartedly to make herself amiable to all, and always clung as well as she could to the thresholds of Holy Church. She stored up the precepts of Holy Scripture in the depths of her heart, often repeating this prayer, that she 'might dwell in the house of the Lord all the days of her life', and might see and work his will.

Her mother died, gripped by bodily sickness and seized by a heavy fever. Then King Didan built a church in the town of Oxford, and had it dedicated in honour of the Holy Trinity, the spotless Virgin Mary and All Saints. Revered Frideswide asked her father, the same King Didan, to give her the church, and he gave her the church. After her mother's death the religious virgin studied to serve God day and night in vigils and prayers, always striving to forget bodily food, and to absorb spiritual food with all her might. Viewing the passing pomp and glory of this word, and valuing it all 'as dung', the virgin Frideswide gave everything that she had to the poor. She always wore a hair-shirt, and her food was a little barley-bread with a few vegetables and water. Meanwhile all the English people marvelled at such virtue in one so young, and the king rejoiced, seeing and understanding that his only daughter was a vessel of the Holy Spirit.

The blessed virgin besought her father, saying

"Sweetest father, help me to become worthy of the nun's habit, to praise and bless God's name forever in his temple." King Didan rejoiced greatly when he heard his daughter, and summoning a certain religious man named Orgar, bishop of Lincoln, he caused him to consecrate his daughter Frideswide to God. With her were also hallowed twelve virgins, all of noble family. Then the same king caused houses suitable for nuns to be built, namely a refectory, a dormitory and a cloister, and assigned religious men to serve them. King Didan also gave the estates and villages of St Mary, and a third part of the city of Oxford, to provide the nuns' food.

So blessed Frideswide, graced with good habits, studied to tame her body and bring her soul to life, after the words of the apostle saying, 'Put to death those parts of you which belong to the earth.' Not long afterwards King Didan took to his bed, seized by a heavy sickness. Distributing his treasure to the poor, he surrendered his soul to God strengthened by the communion of Christ's body. So blessed Frideswide, bride of Christ, bereft of both parents, devoted herself more and more to the Holy Spirit whom she feared. The blessed virgin resolved in her heart to bend her knees a hundred times by day, to mortify her flesh a hundred times by night, beseeching God's mercy.

One night, while her companions slept, she was thus occupied alone in the oratory which she had built for herself. A devil appeared to her, bedecked with gold and silver and every precious stone and surrounded by a flock of demons. He said to her, "My delightful virgin, the time has come to receive the reward of your labours. So come and adore me: for I am Christ, and I shall give you the crown of eternal life which you have earned." "Wretched and most stinking creature", answered blessed Frideswide, " why do you not fear God's judgment? The day is coming when both you and your master will receive eternal punishment. So why do you promise what you do not have?" So saying, the revered virgin signed her body with the standard of the cross, and at once the devil vanished, bellowing and wailing. The blessed virgin, persisting in prayer and steadfast in vigils, was unperturbed.

A certain king of Leicester named Algar, a most villainous man and hateful to God, succeeded to the kingdom after King Didan's death. He sent envoys to blessed Frideswide, saying. "King Algar has sent us to you, virgin Frideswide, wishing to take you in marriage. but if you object he will have you dragged to a brothel." To whom the virgin hallowed for God replied, "I am betrothed to Christ, King of all Kings, so it seems abominable that I should leave the King to obey the commands of a slave. As for your threat to drag me to a brothel, you know that the soul cannot be polluted except by consent of the will. But in any case, 'the Lord is on my side, I have no fear: what can a man do to me?' "

The king's officers indignantly said "Unless you submit willingly to the king's commands, we will seize you and take you to King Algar willy-nilly." When blessed Frideswide heard this she looked upwards, and said in a clear voice. " 'Arise, Lord, give man no chance to boast his strength; summon the nations before thee for judgement; let them know that they are but men.' 'Grasp arms and shield, and rise up to help me: let me hear thee declare, 'I am thy salvation.' ' " As the holy virgin spoke their eyes were struck blind, and they could not 'see the light of heaven'.

When the people of the city of Oxford saw this they fell terrified at the holy virgin's feet, begging her to pray for them. The most holy woman, wishing to return good for ill, knelt and began to pray, saying "Invisible and unchanging God, who made 'heaven and earth, the sea, and all things in them'; who 'formed Adam from the dust of the earth', and who, when he had been seduced by the Devil's envy and expelled from the joy of paradise, redeemed him by the death of your son our Lord Jesus Christ; give back to these wretched men the light of their eyes, so that this people may know that 'thou are compassionate and gracious, forbearing, ever-constant and true', who live and reign world without end." As all replied "Amen" their eyes were restored, and throwing themselves at the blessed virgin's feet they praised the Lord, magnifying his great mercy.

They came to King Algar and recounted all that had happened. Mad with rage and fury, the king said, "Neither her incantations nor her false dogma nor her magic art shall free her from my hands, or prevent me from having her." That night, as blessed Frideswide prayed, an angel of the Lord appeared to her, saying

"Chosen vessel of the Holy Spirit, do not fear the accursed king's threats: Jesus Christ will 'hide you in the shadow of his wings', and his right hand will uphold you. Go to the river, taking with you whichever you wish of your fellow-nuns, and you will find a boat and a boatman provided by God. Get into the boat, and the all-powerful Lord will 'lead you by a straight way' to glorify his name." So saying, he left her.

The blessed virgin arose and called two nuns, virgins dedicated with her to God. When they reached the river Thames as the angel had directed, they found a boat, and

sitting in it a young man with a gleaming, angelic face who thus addressed the virgins, "Step into the boat, hallowed virgins." They got into the boat, and, guided by the Lord, arrived within an hour's space at the town called Bampton. They left the boat, and at once the young man vanished from their sight. Then blessed Frideswide, fearing the wicked king's snares, went with her virgins into a certain wood called Binsey, not far from that town. There they found a path leading to a little hut, built in former times by herdsmen guarding herds of swine, which was completely covered with ivy. The most holy virgin entered it with her virgins, fortifying herself with the sign of the holy cross.

The profane king arose and came with his henchmen to the town of Oxford, intent on defiling the vessel hallowed for God. But as the king entered the city his eyes were struck blind, and he could see nothing. It is thought to have come about in this way that kings never enter Oxford. The profane king remained blind all the days of his life, always plotting and scheming to injure blessed Frideswide. But the blessed virgin of Christ always carried the voice of the gospel in her breast, and never ceased from divine meditations and prayer by day or night. The revered virgin stayed in that wood for about three years.

There was a girl in the same town of Bampton whom a devil had struck blind nearly seven years previously. While she slept one night a man appeared to her in a dream, saying "Go into the wood where the nuns dwell, take the water which falls from blessed Frideswide's hands when she washes them, wipe it on your eyes, and you will recover your sight." When morning came, the girl told her father what she had seen. Holding her hand, the father led her along until they came to the virgin's dwelling. He waited for the time when blessed Frideswide washed her hands; then, taking the water, he wiped it on his daughter's eyes, and at once she recovered her sight. So they blessed God and returned home, praising the Saviour's omnipotence and recounting the wonders which they had seen holy Frideswide work.

There was a certain youth named Alward in the village called Seacourt who chopped wood with an axe on Sunday, unheeding the day of the Lord's Resurrection. While he was thus occupied his hand stuck to the haft, so that he was completely unable to bend his fingers, but cried out in a loud voice that his hand was burning. He was led to the holy virgin, and falling at her feet began to plead for her help. Brimming over with pity, she knelt, moved by compassion, and began to ask for the Lord's mercy, saying "Adonäi, Lord God, great and wonderful, who appeared to Moses 'in the flame of a burning bush', and gave him the law in Sinai, and led the Children of Israel from the land of Egypt, and made them pass dry-footed through the midst of the Red Sea; and who brought the prophet Jonah safe and sound from the whale's belly, and willed your son our Lord Jesus Christ to be incarnate for the world's redemption; I beseech you, by this invocation, to restore this man to his former health, because you are the blessed God, saviour of all who hope in you, world without end." As the bystanders replied "Amen" the virgin made the sign of the cross and, holding the youth's hand, freed him and banished his pain. Returning home, he glorified God. So blessed Frideswide's name was spread through the whole region to the Lord's praise.

It happened that some fishermen, in the manner of

such folk, got into a boat one night to catch fish. They put their nets into the boat and fell asleep there, when one of them was seized by a demon. He began to laugh madly, and grabbing one of his companions strangled him with his hands, and would have torn him apart with his teeth. The others held him, tied his hands behind him, and led him to the blessed virgin's oratory. Seeing God's image mocked by the devil, the revered virgin knelt and prayed to the Lord, that through the strength of the Holy Spirit he would free his creation laid low by the enemy of mankind. So saying, she made the sign of the holy cross on his forehead and said, "Satan, depart from the image which God made in his own likeness." As she spoke he became as though dead, and fell to the ground. The blessed virgin ordered him to be unbound. When he was free, she held his hand and said. " 'In the name of Jesus Christ of Nazareth, arise unharmed." And he got up in his right mind, and began to glorify God who had freed him through the merits of holy Frideswide. His name was Leowin. The Lord worked this and many other miracles through blessed Frideswide.

One day she said to her companions, "Let us return to our monastery." So a boat was made ready, the blessed virgins embarked, and coming to the city of Oxford they were received with honour by the citizens and all the clergy. Blessed Frideswide had just entered the town when a young man full of leprosy ran up to her and said, "I beseech you, virgin Frideswide, to give me a kiss in the name of Jesus Christ." Filled as she always was with the

Holy Spirit, she made the sign of the cross and gave him a kiss in the Lord's name, and at once he was cleaned of his leprosy. Seeing what good works and miracles were done by holy Frideswide, the people and all the clergy of the town rejoiced at her coming.

So the blessed virgin of Christ never ceased from serving almighty God, and she mortified her body to bring her soul to life. When this had continued for a long time, the day of repayment drew near when she would receive from the Lord the reward of her labours. On 12 October an angel of the Lord appeared to her, saying "19 October will be a Sunday, and you will receive from the Lord the crown of eternal life for which you have always longed. Because you disdained your father's earthly palace, a heavenly hall is prepared for you, and unquenchable light." So saying, the angel left her.

Then the most blessed virgin Frideswide was seized with a violent fever, and as bodily sickness grew her limbs began to fail. So one day all the citizens of that town came to her, and the blessed virgin ceaselessly edified them with wholesome advice. When the Saturday came on whose morrow she was to depart from her body, she asked for a grave to be opened for her in the church of the blessed Mary mother of God, saying "Tomorrow will be Sunday, and I do not wish for anyone to work on my account. For tonight, after the third cock-crow, I shall go to my Lord strengthened by Christ's body and blood. 'I have fought the good fight; I have finished the course' of justice; I have despised the world and all its pomp;

therefore 'the garland of righteousness awaits me.'' Thus she spoke; and as the pain of sickness grew, she asked for the eucharist of Christ to be brought to her. Joyfully receiving it, she began to bless almighty God.

When greatly burdened by the weight of sickness, as she had foretold, she looked upwards after much preaching and said in a clear voice, "Welcome, holy virgins, welcome". The bystanders asked her with whom she was speaking, but she replied "Do you not see the blessed virgions of God, Catherine and Cecily?" She spoke to them further and then said for all to hear, "Now I come, my Lord," After the third cock-crow, as she had foretold, she bade everyone farewell and passed to the Lord Jesus Christ. In that hour such a light blazed through the whole city of Oxford, and such a sweet scent filled it for three hours, that all marvelled and glorified God.

A certain man stricken with paralysis, a very rich man, ordered his servants to carry him to the holy virgin's grave. When they had borne him to the grave he regained his full health on the spot through the merits of holy Frideswide, and he who for two years had been dumb and lame, carried by the hands of others, walked home on his own feet praising God.

Another named Athelwold, a nobleman, who was crippled from the navel downwards, came to the church door while they were burying blessed Frideswide's body, dragging his body on two crutches. He wanted to enter the church, but became of the crowd of people he could not. But he began to shout at the church door, "Chosen bride of Christ, virgin Frideswide, free me from my infirmities. For I know that if you want to help me, you can ." So saying, he became as well as if he had never had any sickness. Rising and leaping up, and bounding like a stag, he entered the church manfully, holding up in his hands the crutches on which he had formerly dragged his body, praising God the redeemer of all.

The blessed virgin Frideswide passed to the Lord on 19 October in the year from the Lord's incarnation 727. She was buried in St Mary's church, on the south side, where many miracles have been worked on account of her merits by our Lord Jesus Christ, who with the Father and the Holy Spirit lives and reigns world without end, Amen.

III

The Binsey Episode
(from 'Life B', c. 1150)

The author of 'Life B", who omits the name of the wood near Bampton where the nuns hide, instead inserts this additional chapter between the miracle of the blind girl of Bampton and the miracle of the young man of Seacourt:

She called together the companions of her seclusion and said , "I think that this is the right time to return nearer to our own monastery. For either through their usual concern for us, or falling into the abyss of grief in our absence, our sisters might (which God forbid) have strayed from the right path." Thus she spoke; and when a boat had been made ready, and she and her companions had embarked, it went swiftly and surely by the boatmen's strength to the estate called Binsey near the city. Disembarking and surveying the scene, she decided that it would be useful to stay for a short while outside the city and devote themselves to sweet tranquility. The virgins whom she had left in the monastery would not find it troublesome to come there, and it would be less exposed to the townsfolk, always looking for some fresh novelty. On that estate was a place entangled with various kinds of trees, called Thornbury in the Saxon tongue because of the many different species of thorns there, lonely and most suitable for devotion. Here she straightway built an oratory, and many buildings well-suited to the needs of holy people. And since the branch of the river was some way away, and she felt it inconvenient for the sisters to go there to draw water, she obtained by her prayers a well which remains to this day, and performs healing works for many who drink from it.* Here she hoped to hide, here devote herself to sweet tranquility and shun the crowds.

* *another manuscript reads* . . . for many praying there.

ST MARGARET'S CHURCH, BINSEY

‑✦➤‑✦➤‑✦➤‑✦➤‑✦➤‑✦➤‑✦➤‑✦➤‑✦➤‑◄✦‑◄✦‑◄✦‑◄✦‑◄✦‑◄✦‑◄✦‑◄✦‑◄✦‑

Acrostic Verse on St Frideswide

Bodleian MS Digby 177 f. 320ᵛ, written in a
14th-century hand

F ontem in sicco fundo a Domino impetravit
R egibus Oxonie iter opturavit
I uvenem leprosum osculo mundavit
D emonem in specie Cristi superavit
E dgarum regem Leyces' lumine privavit
S ecuris manubrium a manu liberavit
V isum dedit militibus quos prius excecavit
V irgini Bamptonie lumen restauravit
I n silva per triennium cum Sponso habitavit
D ementem ligatum penitus liberavit
A ngelo ductore Bamptonie navigavit.

F rom the dry earth she brought a fountain springing;
R oads she barred at Oxford to kings who came riding;
I n her gentle kiss the leper found cleansing;
D emon in the guide of Christ she defeated;
E dgar of Leicester at her word was blinded.
S pellbound the hand held the axe till she freed it.
W arriors she had blinded, she healed; planted vision
I n the blind girl's eyes; to the lunatic gave reason;
D welt three years in the woods with her Saviour.
A ngels brought her safely to Bampton by the river.

(Translated by Anne Ridler)